D1550630

Classic American BICYCLES

Jay Pridmore
in collaboration with the
Bicycle Museum of America, New Bremen, Ohio

BICYCLE BOOKS®
FROM
MBI Publishing Company

First published in 1999 by MBI Publishing Company, 729 Prospect Avenue, PO Box 1, Osceola, WI 54020-0001 USA

MBI Publishing Company books are also available at discounts in bulk quantity for industrial or sales-promotional use. For details write to Special Sales Manager at Motorbooks International Wholesalers & Distributors, 729 Prospect Avenue, PO Box 1, Osceola, WI 54020-0001 USA.

Library of Congress Cataloging-in-Publication Data Available

ISBN 1-58068-001-1

On the front cover: The Black Phantom became the fantasy ride of kids from 1949 through most of the 1950s. The Phantom won children's hearts with chrome, chrome, and more chrome. Red and Green Phantoms were available for kids to express individuality, but the Black Phantom was king of the playground.

On the frontispiece: A funny bike becomes a classic: 1973 Apple Krate

On the title page: By trying to keep up with Schwinn, many manufacturers came up with their own unique ideas. Looking similar to the Black Phantom, the Roadmaster Luxury Liner was a high-end kids' bike that was a big deal just to own. It combined a new rear brakelight, bowed struts around each wheel, and a suspension system that rivaled Frank Schwinn's "knee-action" fork.

On the back cover: On the left is a 1934 Elgin Blackhawk from the Columbia Manufacturing Company, and on the right is a 1936 Shelby Speedline Airflo from the Shelby Cycle Co. The Blackhawk was a decked-out beauty with electric light, speedometer, and prominent horn. It wasn't particularly streamlined, but it featured accessories for every childhood fascination. The Airflo featured graceful curves down to the fender braces, "teardrop" pedals, and one of the most extravagant horn tanks of the day.

Edited by Sara Nelson
Designed by Dan Perry

Printed in Hong Kong

Contents

Acknowledgments

The majority of the bicycles pictured in this book are from the collection of the Bicycle Museum of America, New Bremen, Ohio. This museum was founded in 1997 by Jim Dicke and now represents one of the leading collections of antique and classic bicycles in the United States. Mr. Dicke, Curator Annette Thompson, and the museum's researcher Dee Fledderjohn have been indispensable in writing and assembling this book. The author thanks them profusely.

The photographs of the Museum's collection are the work of Jeff Hackett, of Orange, Connecticut. Hackett is a leading photographer of classic cars, motorcycles, and bicycles. His work for this book speaks for itself; his creativity and eye were crucial ingredients in the visual content of Classic American Bicycles.

Others whose help has been important in preparing this book include Richard Schwinn of Waterford Bicycles, bicycle writer Jim Langley of Santa Cruz, California; Mark Mattei of Cycle Smithy, Chicago; the National Mountain Bike Hall of Fame and Museum in Crested Butte, Colorado; and the National Bicycle Dealers Association, Costa Mesa, California.

Introduction
Classic Bikes Forever!

As we look ahead to the technological future, it is exciting and interesting to imagine the role that bicycles could play. Bikes have the potential to relieve urban congestion. They can help make us healthier. They keep the air cleaner. Bicycles are certainly good things, and they're fascinating contraptions, too. With fancy metals, intricate suspension, elegant gearing, and other design features, there are a lot of reasons to get excited about the bicycles of the twenty-first century.

Over one hundred years ago, people were talking about the bicycles of the future, too. By the 1880s, velocipedes, as they were called, represented the most advanced technology of the period. They were also a powerful social force. Bicycles ushered in mass productivity in America, helped liberate women, even advanced the cause of democracy. A little later, they amused the heck out of kids when kids ruled the roost. Each contribution of the bicycle represents a great story. Taken together, they're quite an epic indeed.

Maybe that's what underlies the current fascination with antique and classic bikes—the long and basically happy history bicycles have enjoyed. It is a history that includes the high-wheeler era when social lions rode with socialists, sharing the thrill of propelling themselves six feet above the pavement. It also includes the early safety bikes of the 1890s, a time when some smart inventors got involved in bicycle development, including the Wright brothers and Henry Ford.

By 1900, the story of bicycles was overshadowed by the newer and faster age of motorcycles and automobiles. But bicycles never went away. In the first decades of the twentieth century, bicycle racing was one of America's most prominent spectator sports, and some of the nation's biggest heroes were cyclists. One of them, Major Taylor, was black, and through cycling he helped chip away at the hard racial barriers of his era.

The bicycle later received a needed jump-start during the Depression, when balloon-tire bikes were developed and youngsters everywhere took to bumping them around their neighborhoods. Bicycles also struck the fancy of industrial designers of the art deco age, and they showed that hardly any invention represented such a blend of form, function, and, perhaps most important, fantasy. Bicycles could evoke motorcycles or even rocket ships of the imagination.

Draisine, ca. 1816

Baron von Drais de Saverbrun, Germany
In one form or another, the bicycle has been appearing for centuries. One of the first functioning two-wheelers was devised in Germany by Baron von Drais, a landscape gardener and keeper of forests for the powerful Duke of Baden. Despite limitations, it led to the next step of French carriage makers who took the critical step of attaching cranks to the axle and inventing something they called the *veloce* in the 1860s.

Bicycles have remained a durable part of the social landscape. This is because they are so marvelously versatile. Early on, they were ridden by courting couples, by ambulance drivers, by infantrymen, and even by street-sweeping brigades. And they have always had an ability to change with the times. Witness the muscle bike era, which began in the 1960s, when kids concocted 20-inch frames, polo seats, and ape-hanger handlebars. To say Sting-Rays were well-suited to a generation of American kids would be an understatement. In the 1970s, the energy crisis made ten-speeds the perfect solution, even among adults who would no sooner race than make romance on a tandem. When that boom puttered out, another trend was in the offing: mountain bikes.

Mountain bikes represent one of the more fascinating chapters of bicycle history, perhaps because they touch so many interesting social and historical themes. The mountain bike story combines balloon-tire "clunkers" and athletic hippies who loved the outdoors as much as they loved bicycles. The creators started with rusty old frames that they found in junkyards, and by force of imagination, created an industry of high-performance machines with fancy steel and geometric precision. This speaks well for the bikers, but it speaks very well for the original bikes as well.

Maybe this is why classic bikes took off. The original mountain bikers knew that the balloon-tired, heavy-framed old bikes of the 1930s were durable. Then they took a second look and realized that the Aerocycles and Airflos and Luxury Liners of the balloon-tire era were among the most dashing consumer products of their age.

Collectibles depend upon emotion, and the modern adults who collect old bikes are nothing if not nostalgic. Black Phantoms return them to their streets where stickball was a big deal and Cyclelocks were all the security one needed. Today, financial planners and actuaries remember their first wheelie on their first muscle bike. Old ballooners and not-quite-as-old Sting-Rays are now going for thousands of dollars, all to recapture some of the thrill of youth!

There are left-brain aspects to bicycle history as well. Bicycles freed women from the corset. They led directly to the automotive age. Six-day racers recall days when gangsters and celebrities rubbed shoulders in the Jazz Age. The streamline

Boneshaker, late 1870s
J. Shire & Co., Detroit
Boneshakers were aptly named. This version of the French-devised *veloce* showed skill in the wheelwright's art, but less of an understanding of optimal bicycle geometry, not to mention gearing, which was another decade in coming.

era was defined as much by balloon-tired bicycles as by soda fountains in drug stores.

It's not too much to say that bicycles have changed the way we live. A hundred years ago, they helped bring together neighborhoods and social classes. Thirty years ago, they closed the gap between adults driving GTOs and kids pedaling the next best thing. And recently, bikes have saved us, or some of us, from the hordes who clog the streets with fumes during rush hour.

Bikes may be the last place technology actually enhances our independence. What else is there?. . . Cars? Hardly. Airplanes? No way. Computers? We're not sure. But bikes are pure, optimistic, and healthful. Life is good on a bike. It always was. That's why they remain so popular, and it's why the old ones, the classics, represent something that we are paying dearly to preserve, collect, and somehow recapture.

Chapter 1
America Discovers the Bicycle

By the 1880s, many of the greatest technical minds in America were at work perfecting the bicycle. But the greatest bicycle man of the era was not a mechanic, a metallurgist, nor even much of a cyclist. He was Colonel Albert A. Pope, factory man par excellence and a central figure in the social and commercial phenomenon called the "bicycle boom."

Colonel Pope founded the company that built America's first production bicycle, the Columbia. He was a major force behind campaigns to develop stronger rims, tighter spokes, softer suspension, and a score of other technical improvements. Had he been active earlier, Pope might have gone into farm machinery. Had he come later, he'd have found his way into automobiles or maybe telephones. But in Pope's prime, the market was demanding one thing from technology above all, and that was bicycles. As the man behind Columbia, he had the vision and courage to both create this business and rise to the top of it.

Pope's first real exposure to bicycles came in 1876 during his visit to the Philadelphia Centennial Exposition. High-wheel "ordinaries," as they were later called, were on display as part of manufacturing exhibits from England, where bicycles were already flourishing nicely. As Pope watched riders glide effortlessly around the fair grounds, he was intrigued by the potential of the American market, where bicycles like this were relatively unknown.

Pope was in the shoe industry at the time, doing well as a merchant of "fittings and findings" to the trade. But shoes must have seemed mundane to the Civil War veteran. More than most people, the Colonel foresaw the coming of larger machine-driven factories. He envisioned the grandeur of mass production. Most of all, perhaps, he imagined bicycles on every paved street in America.

Columbia Expert, 1883
Pope Manufacturing Co., Hartford, Connecticut
Pope's Columbia factory produced the most advanced bicycles of the day. They were relatively simple, all the better for Pope's objective of mass production. The Expert's front wheel is 58 inches in diameter. Its metal tubing is nickel-plated to avoid scratches. Hubs, ball bearings, rims, and other essentials were fabricated in the former sewing machine factory that Pope made into one of the most advanced mass-production facilities in the country at the time.

Victor, 1892
Overman Wheel Co., Chicopee Falls, Massachusetts
By the time this Victor was built, the safety bicycle was in production, and high wheelers were for the dedicated and brave. Despite its old-fashioned character at the time, this one boasted obviously advanced features. Tangential spokes were self-tightening as the wheel rolled forward. Brakes were machined by modern metal-working equipment. Less technological but critical to the rider was the strategic placement of a peg above the rear wheel for relatively trouble-free mounting.

Victor Safety, 1889 (left)
Overman Wheel Co., Chicopee Falls, Massachusetts
American Safety, 1887 (right)
Gormully & Jeffery, Chicago
In the late 1880s, different designs were produced to expand the bicycle's usefulness by making it safer—well, at least safer than mounting a 60-inch high-wheeler. The crucial idea was for more efficient transmission, which Gormully & Jeffery (later makers of Ramblers) achieved with a system of treadles (right). Shortly thereafter, however, the chain drive was relatively mastered. In the Victor Safety (left), the Overman company even added a suspension system to make the ride not just safer but more comfortable as well.

Old Hickory, 1897
Tonk Manufacturing Co., Chicago

As soon as Pope returned home to Boston, he hired a blacksmith to make a high-wheel prototype. It was heavy, expensive, and so distinctly unsaleable that the Colonel decided to get into the market first as an importer. By 1878, however, he was turning out America's first native-built bicycle, modeled after a relatively simple English high-wheeler, the Duplex Excelsior made by Bayliss, Thomas & Co.

Within a few years, Pope moved his bicycle concern to a former sewing machine factory in Hartford and established one of the premier manufacturing operations in the country. It had "158 different machines [which] perform their automatic labor," as described in an 1882 article in *Frank Leslie's*

Popular Monthly. Die-making and ball-bearing assembly were elevated to an art form. "In the wheel room the wheels are set up and trued; in the tiring room the rubber tires, now made in molds, are stretched upon the rims, cemented and baked; in the assembling room, the wheels, forks, and backbones are put together, and every part duly marked and tagged."

There were few other examples of mass production of this scale at this time, and the precision practiced by Pope Manufacturing Company in forging, machining, and finishing the scores of interchangeable parts was unprecedented. Publications of the day lavished praise on the owner. He employed able lieutenants, admitted the magazine *Bicycling World* some years later, "but the aortal valve of the business, the pistonic dynamic force of the Pope scheme, was Col. Albert A. Pope himself."

At least one of Pope's "pistons" drove a publicity machine, and in 1882 he financed an illustrated monthly, *The Wheelman*, which remained one of the foremost sporting magazines of the era. One of the *Wheelman*'s early projects was to finance Englishman Thomas Stevens on a round-the-world journey by bicycle, chronicled everywhere and followed by cyclists and non-cyclists alike.

Another of Pope's pistons, maybe the overactive one, was dedicated to the not-so-gentle art of litigation. It seemed "in those days that the patent attorney was more important than the inventor or improver," opined *Bicycling World*. Thus, Pope patented every aspect of his bicycles, and he bought patents on improvements belonging to others. He even found a patent for a basic velocipede, granted to an obscure French

Chilion ladies' hickory model, 1898
M. D. Stebbins Manufacturing Co., Springfield, Massachusetts
In the 1890s, the wild popularity of bicycles led to hundreds of makers and thousands of innovations. One interesting variation on the standard metal technology was the use of hickory in the frame. Hickory was well-nigh unbreakable, said the makers, and a good shock absorber as well. More to the point, perhaps, was the elegance of polished wood and ornamental lugs. The Tonk Manufacturing Co.'s Old Hickory (left), in particular, provided its rider with a measure of vehicular prestige.

immigrant, Pierre Lallement, in 1866 and relatively forgotten until Pope bought it and enforced it with a vengeance.

The Lallement patent expired in 1883. After that, the expansion of bicycle producers accelerated, but so did the lawsuits. Every possible design feature or accessory was subject to litigation. Saddle styles were dragged through the courts. Brakes, bearings, handlebars, lamps, and many other details of the bicycle were all subject to a blizzard of patent work and legal activity.

Colonel Pope usually prevailed in these matters, but he met his match in the courtroom with a Chicopee Falls, Massachusetts, manufacturer named Albert H. Overman. Overman had many commercial abilities, and his Victor line quickly became a leading name in the bicycle trade—a credit in no small part to his own lawyers who defended the Victor's innovations and attacked those of others. Lighter rims was one Overman development. A way of crimping solid rubber tires in a formed rim was another.

Unpleasant as they were, these patent fights may have led to better bicycles. "We can now see that this competition was the breath of life to cycling," commented *Bicycling World*, taking the historical view a few

Columbia Century, 1893

Pope Manufacturing Co., Hartford, Connecticut
By 1887, Pope Manufacturing was using the rear-wheel-drive concept, which revolutionized bicycles. As the safety bicycle expanded the market, developments were fast in coming. The double-diamond frame was evolving, and it would remain the standard bicycle design more or less permanently. In the Century, Pope also used what was called the "elliptical" front sprocket, devised for maximum power, which anticipated something Shimano called a "Biopace" chain ring in the 1980s.

years later. "Without it the pace would have been much more snail-like."

The next major development of the bicycle came in the middle 1880s—the safety bicycle. High-wheelers were frankly treacherous, and more so as riders sought larger wheels for greater riding efficiency, some as large as 60 inches in diameter. Thus, the idea of gears, chain, and two wheels of equal size represented a major advance. The safety bicycle came from England, but Pope, Overman, and other competitors quickly took it up and did what they could to improve and patent it. Both devised elaborate suspension systems—the Columbia with springs near the hub of the front wheel, the Victor with an elliptical front fork, and many others with elaborate springs under the saddle.

Before the 1880s were over, another important development arrived, again from Great Britain. This was the pneumatic tire, invented by Irish veterinarian John B. Dunlop. Patent-mad Pope and Overman tried to ignore the air-filled tire at first (on the theory, presumably, that they couldn't control it). This gave other manufacturers, notably Chicago's Gormully & Jeffery, the opportunity to distinguish themselves with innovative tubes, treads, and other features.

Along with these improvements came the "double diamond" frame—the sturdiest design yet—which evolved without ever being patented but became the standard design for the next 100 years. Thus perfected, bicycles now had a pervasive effect on American society: people of all kinds were mobile, both geographically and socially. It was the beginning of the first true bicycle boom.

"The bicycle is the most democratic of all vehicles," wrote Charles Pratt, author of the first major book on the subject, *The American Bicycler*. Pratt, a lawyer and editor who worked for Pope, also advanced a movement that had been developing for some time: bicycle clubs. Clubs had been growing on their own for some time, established to organize regular Sunday rides to rustic taverns in the countryside. Pratt undertook to assemble many such clubs under the umbrella of the League of American Wheelmen (L.A.W.).

By the mid-1890s, the L.A.W. had become a major national organization with a membership of over 100,000. With such numbers, and with a passionate and distinctly egalitarian membership, there grew the temptation for the L.A.W. to dabble in politics. League officials often voiced their overriding concern, "good roads," which was also adopted as the name of the organization's journal.

Politicians of the period were always careful to curry favor of cycling clubs. In New York, Mayor Robert Van Wyck kept an 1887 promise to cyclists and established a street-cleaning brigade to clear the roads of obstacles that could endanger wheelmen. In Chicago, Carter Harrison Jr. won the mayoral election in 1899 on the strength of a better-roads campaign.

Politically speaking, middle-of-the-road populists held sway in bicycledom. But it is interesting that in Boston during this period, the Young Socialists took up cycling and toured the countryside wearing blazing red jerseys and distributing literature. On the other side of the spectrum,

Illinois Cycling Club Headquarters, Chicago, ca. 1890s
Cycling was considered uplifting and democratic as clubs proliferated throughout the United States. High-wheel cycles retained a certain exclusivity, because of the expense and skill involved in riding them. The safety bicycle brought "wheeling" to a more truly egalitarian level, and even added women to the fraternity of cyclists.

the editor of *Good Roads* once took the cudgel for the gold standard and against "free silver"—this being the view of business interests—but cycling never really became identified with highly partisan questions.

Women's liberation, perhaps the biggest issue of this period, was very much associated with the bicycle boom. Because of its inherent dangers, high-wheel riding was uncommon for women in the early days of the bicycle. Later it was of questionable taste for the "weaker sex" to ride safety bicycles. But attitudes were changing. Women were soon suiting up to ride, and

Lady's New Star, 1897
New Star Company, Smithfield, New Jersey
By the 1890s, many different approaches were devised for the peaking bicycle market. The idea behind the New Star (above) was that women might prefer treadles and a leather belt to pedals and a greasy chain. For his part, Mr. Carroll tempted the bicycle buyer with a third sprocket (right). Whatever trial and error these fine-looking bicycles represented, the trusty chain was never really replaced.

manufacturers followed their lead with the "drop frame" for easier mounting and dismounting.

There were attempts to keep women off bicycles, though none were organized. In Chicago's Lincoln Park, one ill-starred gent witnessed a matron *en biciclette* and "hooted" loudly, according to court records. The rider instantly registered a complaint with the constabulary, and the man was arrested, hauled into court, fined a small sum, and scolded. People who preferred corsets were naturally against female wheeling, since bicycles were incompatible with such attire. Those offended by bloomers (wide-legged pantaloons regarded as modern) could only shield their eyes from women who wore them astride safety bicycles

Even Frances Willard, whose brand of feminism led to her founding of the Women's Christian Temperance Union, wrote a book on the virtues of women cycling. On the theory that conservative voices were most effective at advancing risky new causes, Willard's endorsement was credited with breaking the floodgates in favor of women and bicycles.

Part of the debate against cycling, and in particular cycling by females, was based on health claims. Bicycling seemed custom-made for the new breed of physicians and pseudo-physicians adept at serious descriptive phrases and basic quackery. One warned of "posterior dorsal curvature" as a distinct risk of cycling. Another claimed that it promoted "heating of the blood in women," with the solution that something called Payne's Celery Tonic could counteract such ills, though its only sure effect was to separate the wheelwoman from her money.

The fundamental healthfulness of cycling was not ignored, of course, and Pope's publication reserved some of its highest fees for doctors and others who could write convincingly of its positive effects. One medically-inclined writer stated that cycling could "equalize matters in respect to the general size of the body," thus wheeling could produce benefits for the overly stout and the overly trim. Another

Carroll Gear-to-Gear, 1897
Thomas A. Carroll, Philadelphia

Punnett Companion, 1897
Punnett Cycle Manufacturing, Rochester, New York
The romance of the bicycle was obvious from the moment it hit the streets. Bicycles enabled young couples to escape the gaze and scrutiny of their neighborhoods, and the development of tandems was a direct response to market need. How to fill that need was not quite so clear. Early on, inventors were committed to the side-by-side approach. Problems in the Punnett (above) and the Wolff-American (right) were obvious, however. Extraordinary balance was required in one. In both, the steering called for a harmony of wills. Welcome to marriage, the manufacturers seemed to be saying.

reported the results of research that found cycling to be advantageous when practiced by patients in mental hospitals.

Cycling's hold on the public imagination in the 1890s also lifted bicycle racing to prominence both as recreation and as a spectator sport. Racing began nearly as soon as bicycles appeared on the streets. Initially, it was disorganized. The annual

Pullman Race of Chicago, for example, began in 1883, and often featured chaos at the start, the "odor of fraud" at the finish, and interest on the part of nearly everyone in the city. Riders came in all shapes and sizes, and the spectacle was certainly more memorable than the eventual winner.

Given this enthusiasm, it was not long before commercial concerns took an interest

Wolff-American Companion, 1898
R. H. Wolff & Co., New York

in racing. Pope, Overman, and many other manufacturers made arrangements with top racers to ride their wheels. While the moralistic L.A.W. eagerly discouraged professionalism, their editorializing against money proved to be futile.

Early racing, which took place on dirt tracks, produced some indisputable heroes. To ride Victors, for example, Overman hired George Hendee, who won the first national cycling championship in 1882 in Boston. (Hendee was later the developer of the Indian motorcycle.) A younger upstart, W. A. Rowe, rode Columbias for Pope. Certainly the dazzle of any race featuring these two overshadowed the taint of professionalism. When Rowe finally defeated Hendee in a major race at Springfield, Massachusetts, in 1887, it was reported that many spectators were weeping, so moved were they by the impact and sportsmanship of the event.

Racing increased in popularity when it shifted to safety bicycles and moved to fast wooden tracks with banked turns. An early champion, and one of the first to race on safety bicycles, was Arthur A. Zimmerman. "Zimmy" drew enthusiastic crowds wherever he raced, and, while still an "amateur," was paid lavishly in jewelry and real estate. The press loved Zimmy, who would violate training by smoking big cigars and staying out late with writers. None of this, however, detracted from his reputation or his ability to prevail in short-distance races and furious sprints that were decided by fractions.

Competitive cycling had other sides, too, such as six-day racing, which in the 1890s was an individual (not a two-man) event. In six-days, cyclists were as durable as they were daft, racing for a full six days with just a few hours rest per day. Spectators and gamblers came and went over the course of the race, which became a social event as well as an athletic one. Newspapers naturally enjoyed promoting "the single sixes." *The New York Times* described "whirling demons who ride between walls of shrieking faces." Promoters gave the writers plenty of off-track fodder, too, such as the infield marriage of one Chicago racer during a rest period; he wore a suit of pink and white tights for the ceremony.

Single sixes were phased out because the best racers were involved in more stately and less debilitating track racing events. These were elite athletes by any standard, and their lives provided poignant insights into American society at large. Which leads to the story of Marshall "Major" Taylor, a black racer who was near the top of the game for a decade.

Taylor's career began around 1896 when he joined a professional circuit, and at first he was little more than an agreeable novelty in the sport. When he began competing for championships, however, his presence definitely ignited racial hostility. (He was banned from racing in Southern cities under any circumstances.)

Taylor's story rivals that of other black sports heroes. He was sometimes treated poorly by other riders who would "pocket" him and prevent him from breaking out of the pack. Normally stoic, Taylor was not reluctant to jostle back when other riders got too close. Despite all, he raced and won major races at New York's Manhattan Beach and New Jersey's Asbury Park in his second year, and by then, most of his opponents regarded him with the respect that he deserved.

But Taylor's was a hard life. He was forced to race internationally, because of continued obstacles in his own country. He won a title in Montreal that made him, it's said, the first black American to win a world championship of any kind. But the lesson of Major Taylor is that his career came too soon. In his own time, racism was too strong and too vile. Despite periods of prosperity, Taylor faded from the scene and died in obscurity, and today his name is unknown outside cycling.

The bicycle assumed a central position in other aspects of society as well. Notably, it drew the most creative technical minds of the time. These included the Duryea brothers, bicycle makers who later turned out the first production automobile in America, and Henry Ford, who

Pierce Arrow, 1900

George N. Pierce, Buffalo, New York

By 1900, the bicycle market was flooded and many manufacturers could see that the bicycle boom was over. But that didn't stop some inventive ones from developing high-end cycles, such as the Pierce Arrow, with drive shaft and telescopic shock—ideas that would later drive George Pierce's successful foray into automobiles (the invention that would draw the curtain on the bicycle era, at least for a while).

Schwinn Quintuplet, 1896
Arnold, Schwinn & Co., Chicago
As racing grew to dimensions that only professional sports can, it also helped advance bicycle technology.
"Multicycles" such as the "quint" above of all kinds were devised, in part, as pace cycles to "draft" for
racers behind.

Iver Johnson Truss-Bridge, 1910
Iver Johnson's Arms and Cycle Works, Fitchburg, Massachusetts
Iver Johnson's company developed lighter tubing and ultimately the "truss bridge" frame while it was the sponsor and mechanical force behind the great racer Major Taylor. The theory then (as it is now) was that what was good for racers was also good for serious cyclists who did not happen to be racing.

was a bicycle mechanic who veered into internal combustion.

Of course, the most interesting bicycle men of the period were a pair of mechanics with an inconspicuous shop in Dayton, Ohio. Orville and Wilbur Wright loved cycling and made a decent business of repairing and

building them. Their top-of-the-line model was a $65 Van Cleve, turned out in 1896, with brazed frames, hubs of their own design, and high-end components.

The Wrights produced only about 150 of these models and made little profit on them. In fact, the Van Cleve would probably

Fowler, 1890
Hill & Moffat, Chicago

World, 1916
Arnold, Schwinn & Co., Chicago

In a period when bicycle racing was a major sport for professionals and amateurs alike, "roadsters" for more leisurely riding also exhibited the lines and features of cycles designed for performance on the track. The examples shown on these two pages prove that every model, like every rider, was a little different. The Fowler's upright profile was built more for comfort than speed. The Racycle's sprockets were oversized, but its gear ratio was no different from less-conspicuous bikes. Then, as now, there was a bit of "show" in many bicycles. The World roadster was particularly flashy because it was the one-millionth bicycle manufactured by Schwinn, which would go on to build millions more.The Rambler and the Stormer also featured unique combinations of geometry, wheelbase, and other subtle features, demonstrating that each of the 2,000 American bicycle manufacturers in business at the turn of the century was a little different from the rest.

Racycle Roadster, 1910
Miami Cycle and Manufacturing, Middletown, Ohio

Rambler, 1900
Gormully & Jeffery, Chicago

be forgotten today except for the fact that Orville and Wilbur were focused on another technology that made them among the most important figures of the twentieth century. Their breakthrough came in 1903 when they flew the first airplane at Kitty Hawk, an event for which their bicycle background definitely deserves credit. The lightweight frame was brazed like a bike. The wings were stabilized by spoke wire. The dual propellers were driven by trusty chains. Even the Wrights' aerodynamic calculations were made with wind vanes mounted on the handlebars of a bike.

There is something poignant about the connection between bicycles and airplanes. It demonstrates how bicycles were overshadowed by other inventions. But without the enormous energy that went

Stormer, 1899
Acme Manufacturing Co., Reading, Pennsylvania

into the bicycle, many inventions and ideas of the twentieth century—from the automobile to women's suffrage—might have developed more slowly. History proves that the madness America held for the bicycle for a decade and a half was a very important madness indeed.

Chapter 2
The Balloon-Tire Revival

In 1934, the national trade association of bicycle manufacturers put on an exhibit at the Century of Progress world's fair in Chicago. There were many bicycle press articles written about it, and by reading between the lines, one could sense the industry's desperation. It was still the Depression, and bike makers were counting on a drop in auto registrations, hoping that two-wheelers might enjoy a resurgence at the motorcar's expense.

There was good reason for despair in the bicycle industry. Just after the turn of the century, the invention had been completely overshadowed by the automobile. Bicycles earned little respect and even fewer sales in the intervening decades, and the majority of bicycle makers either left the trade or moved into cars—Pierces, Ramblers, Wintons, and of course Fords were being made by former bicycle men.

Technically and aesthetically, there was little to recommend bicycles in the first three decades of the twentieth century.

There was hardly any craftsmanship involved—they were usually assembled from parts purchased from many sources. Adults had little interest in them, since cars and motorcycles were widely available, and most regarded bicycles as child's transportation.

As the Depression began to ebb, the industry appeared determined to make a comeback. But nowhere in the official literature is there a word about Frank W. Schwinn, which there should have been because in 1934, Schwinn was in the process of saving the industry. The son of Ignaz Schwinn, the founder of Arnold, Schwinn & Co., Frank was 37 at the time. Anyone acquainted with him knew he was a bright engineer who had little patience for the rest of the bicycle trade.

Schwinn believed that bike quality in the United States was disgusting. His company had been making bicycle frames since its founding in 1895, and he knew what he was talking about when he excoriated his industry for lowering product quality to an

B-10E, 1933
Arnold, Schwinn & Co., Chicago
When Frank W. Schwinn designed the first balloon-tire bicycle, he understood that the youngsters who were its riders cared less for speed and more for the trappings of the automotive age—big fenders, for example, and a serious-looking headlight.

30

Shelby Lindy, 1929
Shelby Cycle Co., Shelby, Ohio
Shelby understood the value of celebrity tie-ins very well. When Charles Lindbergh made his name by flying solo across the Atlantic, Shelby knew they could impress kids with a bicycle that evoked the romance, if not the speed, of aviation and flight.

"irreducible minimum." He claimed that the industry's parts makers cared only for volume, retailers cared only for collecting money, and no one was standing up for the integrity of the bicycle. To say that the industry suffered from a lack of vision would have been a compliment.

But Schwinn did have vision. He also had nerve.

After growing up in his dad's factory, he enrolled at Armour Institute (later Illinois Institute of Technology), but quit after realizing there was little they could teach him that he couldn't learn himself, or already

Dayton "Aircrafted," 1935
Huffman Manufacturing Co., Dayton, Ohio
The Huffman family had been a major manufacturer of roadsters and racing cycles back in the bicycle-boom era. When they returned to the bike business in 1934, the balloon-tire era was upon them. To differentiate themselves, the family's Dayton roots suggested the "aircrafted" moniker and the claim that the welding done on these earth-bound cruisers was similar to the assembly of aeroplane frames.

Aerocycle, 1934
Arnold, Schwinn & Co., Chicago
The romance of flight was driving everyone's fantasies in the period between the two world wars. Schwinn spared no detail in building a bike that soared despite its bulk. The Aerocycle's tank— a motorcycle motif—was shaped like the cross section of a wing. Abundant silver paint made it a conspicuous item in any bike shop.

had. And learn he did, as a bicycle maker beside his father, and later as second-in-command when Arnold, Schwinn & Co. was also one of the largest motorcycle makers in the country. Schwinn moved into internal combustion with Excelsiors and Hendersons in the 1910s and 1920s, and Frank helped design some of the most advanced motorcycles of his era.

The Depression forced Schwinn out of motorcycles, which disappointed Frank W. Schwinn but which he used as an opportunity. While other bicycle men hoped that austerity might return bicycles to its former prosperity, Schwinn had no interest in begging for old business. In 1933, he changed the bicycle industry as radically as anyone ever did. He created a whole new market by understanding that kids could love bicycles and parents would buy them if only the industry turned out something both swell and durable.

The Schwinns were always quality-conscious, partly because Ignaz was an Old World craftsman, and partly because strong tubing, sure welds, and torque-resistant designs were key in the motorcycle business. When Schwinn imagined a stronger bicycle, however, it was easier said than done. The standard parts makers offered nothing in support. They were initially unwilling to change the status quo.

So young Schwinn looked toward Europe. As the son of a German immigrant, Schwinn knew that German manufacturers at this time were producing strong bicycles with wide-tread tires and separate inner tubes. For several years by this time, Schwinn had noticed these bicycles during visits with relatives. Finally he purchased a few, shipped them home, took them apart, and embarked on what would become the first bicycle revival in 40 years.

Accomplishing that was an obstacle course, however. For example, where would the tires come from? Manufacturers bluntly refused to make anything other than the standard 28x1-1/2-inch "glorified garden hose," as Schwinn called it. Only when U. S. Rubber concluded Schwinn would get balloon tires by hook or crook did they agree to an initial order.

Elgin Blackhawk, 1934
Columbia Manufacturing Co., Westfield, Massachusetts
Although it came a year after the B-10E, it had much more in terms of precious accessories. This Sears-marketed beauty remained a step behind Schwinn in the drive to streamline, though the big store's Elgin mark made up for lost time a couple of years later when it produced the Bluebird and Skylark.

Then there were the retailers. Schwinn's first balloon-tire model, the 1933 B-10E, was significantly more expensive than cycles sold in chain stores at the time. So Schwinn, in another courageous move, simply bypassed the big stores. He insisted that wholesalers sell exclusively to bike shops, a less-than-stellar category at the time, often located in alleys and engaged in sidelines as handymen. But Schwinn believed that "specialty" stores would take the time to sell a higher-quality

35

Autocycle, 1936

Arnold, Schwinn & Co., Chicago

In 1934, the Aerocycle, costing around $50, seemed too expensive for the fledgling balloon-tire market, but expectations changed along with a new willingness to spend. By 1936, (with the Depression abating) Schwinn's Autocycle was fully decked with accessories that brought the price upwards of $70, and the market embraced the bike and its gadgets in a big way. It made kids feel like they were driving an accessory-laden Ford or Chevy. It also standardized some of the features that Schwinn developed, patented, and sold with great success. The knee-action front spring fork was one. By 1938, the cantilevered frame enhanced the flowing profile of this streamlined bicycle of choice at the time.

Roadmaster, 1941
Cleveland Welding Co., Cleveland
By 1941, most companies had settled on the standard bicycle design. Good paint and a big horn tank were de rigeuer. Practicalities like rideability and a good kickstand came after the war, when a deluge of accessories were necessary to differentiate an avalanche of balloon-tire bikes.

product, and he was right. This was the advent of Schwinn's "authorized-dealer" network, and more immediately, the beginning of the balloon-tire craze, which brought the industry back from near-death.

The bicycle industry owed Frank W. Schwinn plenty. He not only popularized balloon-tires; he excited the overall market with a succession of refinements to enhance the product. He fashioned and patented the front spring fork, adapted from his motorcycle days. He also designed and patented the cantilever frame, more streamlined than the usual bicycle and arguably more stable.

Most important, Schwinn glorified a market that most manufacturers regarded as second-class: kids. Schwinn created grand fantasies with his new bikes. The 1934 Aerocycle evoked aviation in elaborate ways—even the tank was shaped like the cross section of a wing. The following year Autocycles featured all the auto-like accessories that a bicycle could carry. With the right touches, the rider could easily imagine a swift motorized vehicle, despite balloon tires anchored to pavement by a bicycle weighing some 40 pounds.

Schwinn's passion for bicycles became contagious. Many manufacturers showed

Dayton Champion, 1941
Huffman Manufacturing Co., Dayton, Ohio
Ever since the 1936 Safety Streamliner (inspired by that year's Buick sedan), Huffman kept adding distinctive touches to its bikes. The Champion was a top-of-the-line model that accentuated the fashion for a long wheel base and good curves.

that they too were eager to create a new and positive product. Also influential was the popularity of modern design on manufacturing of all kinds in the 1930s. "Streamlining" was the order of the day, and bicycles quickly adopted this kind of treatment.

Take the Huffman Safety Streamliner, made by the people who made Dayton bicycles during the 1890s bicycle boom. The company, once called the Davis Sewing Machine Co., went through bankruptcy in the 1920s before Horace Huffman revived the family business by getting into gas station equipment, which they manufactured and sold. But Huffman and his son Horace Jr. could not resist their first love, bicycles, so as soon as they could, they produced a balloon-tire cruiser.

Elgin Bluebird, 1936
Columbia Manufacturing Co., Westfield, Massachusetts
The use of streamlining was working overtime when the Bluebird was created. It is one of the most unique bicycles of an era when there was no true standard cruiser design. The Bluebird was the top-of-the-line selection in the Sears catalogue that featured far more prosaic bikes on which a little of the Bluebird's élan probably rubbed off.

Partly inspired by Frank Schwinn's success in 1933, the Huffmans asked an in-law, John Clements, to design something distinctive. Clements was then an owner of the Wayne School Bus Company, and while buses weren't exactly streamlined, the designer in Clements had something sleek up his sleeve. Family lore has it that he was looking at the 1936 Buick, a supremely streamlined piece of work, when he created the Huffman Safety Streamliner and Super Streamliner. They had very fancy profiles indeed, down to the ducktailed rear fork and fender. The models were available with Dayton, National, and Huffman head tags. They had the "graceful, sweeping lines of a modern motor car," said the ads. "New, but not 'freakish'. . ."

While balloon-tire models caught on in a big way with many other manufacturers, there was no truly standard design in the 1930s. To the delight of today's collectors,

Elgin Skylark, 1937
Columbia Manufacturing Co., Westfield, Massachusetts
The Skylark was the Sears-sold girl's model to accompany the Bluebird. This kind of handwork had a short life in the bicycle industry. The weight of the Skylark was also a deterrent. But it demonstrates that Sears sold some very pretty machines. Today, it definitely appeals to collectors for whom originality is a positive virtue and the weight of a Sherman tank is no particular crime.

there were many different approaches to balloon-tire bikes in the days before World War II. Moreover, bicycles were more of a handmade undertaking at the time, resulting in a broad, and sometimes even eccentric, design range. If kids were wary of "freakish" bikes in the 1930s, the most extreme designs are highly coveted 60 years later—and among the most eccentric and coveted today are the Elgins.

Elgin was Sears Roebuck's most important head tag at the time. What the big retailer wanted from its suppliers, it got, and Sears obviously wanted something different for its stores. First built by Columbia and later by Murray Ohio, Elgin designs were among the most distinctive of the 1930s, partly because they had to look appealing in catalogues as well as stores. In 1934, the Elgin Blackhawk was a decked-out beauty

Ingo-Cycle, 1936
Borg-Warner Corp., Chicago
Among a broad range of unique designs in the prewar period, the Ingo was off the charts. It was built for a little more than two years by an automotive company that made electrical parts and accessories. It got all sorts of exposure, making something of a hit at the Chicago world's fair in 1934 and later as a featured prop in a Three Stooges movie. It then joined the pantheon of elegant has-beens when the Borg-Warner plant that produced it decided there was more of a future in military gear.

with electric light, speedometer, and prominent horn. It wasn't particularly streamlined, but it featured accessories for every childhood fascination.

When streamlining became a necessity in 1935 or so, Sears bikes became streamlined to the max. The Elgin Bluebird, for example, is one of the most amazing bicycles of the period, looking less like a song-bird and more like something rolling out of a Buck Rogers movie. The speedometer is in the sculpted tank. Fenders ducktail. There's hardly a bump or a right angle in the package. And the Skylark, the girl's Elgin at the time, has unique lines of its own, though neither design caught the fancy of mainstream kids like the more conservative Schwinns.

Silver King Flo-Cycle, 1936
Monark Silver King, Chicago
Monark built car batteries at a time when auto-parts companies provided major outlets for bicycles. Its partner Silver King fabricated aluminum. Their design looked like something ready to fly off the tarmac. This bike was for the sophisticated kids, of whom there were evidently not enough to make the Flo-Cycle a legend in its own time. It would have to wait for collectors, who now feel very warmly indeed toward this shiny steed.

By the middle 1930s, the bike industry was taking on some signs of the old bicycle boom. Another old bike company on the comeback trail was D. P. Harris Hardware and Manufacturing and their Rollfast brand. The Harris firm's strength was in marketing and selling (the bikes were made by others), and by 1934, Rollfast cruisers were everywhere and selling under a multitude of head tags: Keystone, Cadet, Champion, Century, Puritan, Princeton, Peerless, Rex, Black Beauty, Blue Ribbon, Harvard, and others.

Some trade names were connected to chain stores. Others went to independent bike shops. Most lines included Rollfast's standard balloon-tire model, the Motobike Deluxe, streamlined with two curved top tubes, horn tank, and a version of a spring front fork. Also common on Rollfasts were

Shelby Airflo, 1936
Shelby Cycle Co., Shelby, Ohio
If any cycle maker had the wherewithal to compete with Schwinn, it was Shelby. The Airflo proves the point. It was impressive among the kids in the 1930s. Today it stands as one of the classiest vehicles of any kind from the streamlined era.

43

Rollfast V-474, 1940
D. P. Harris Hardware & Manufacturing, New York
By mastering the art of marketing, D. P. Harris made Rollfast a big name among kids when bikes were the way to their hearts. This one assembled many of the most popular features of the early cruiser period, such as front fork suspension and a "torpedo" headlamp. This bike anticipated the baby-boom period when conformity and standardization were key factors in the business. Rollfast was not a big technical innovator, but by the postwar period, the company was rolling along very nicely indeed.

flashy accessories—sirens, torpedo-shaped headlamps, "Texas steer horn" handlebars, chrome forks, and other options. Rollfast marketed their products with relentless promotion, magazine ads, and even a radio show for kids.

Other manufacturers from the period succeeded on the strength of pure design, and among the purest was the Shelby Cycle Company, based in central Ohio. The Shelby Speedline Airflo was the company's top of the line in 1938 (when Shelby displaced

Alfred Letourneur, 1941

The man Frank Schwinn chose when he wanted to generate enthusiasm for adult cycling and lightweight bicycles was Alfred Letourneur. During his attempt at the world speed record, he reached an amazing 108.92 miles per hour. The bicycle that he rode was a souped-up Paramount, which Schwinn was determined to sell to adults who were not speed demons but interested in good bicycles for Sunday riding.

Schwinn for a couple of years as market leader). The Airflo featured exceedingly graceful curves down to the fender braces and "teardrop" pedals, and one of the most extravagant horn tanks of the day.

Shelby didn't rest just on its looks. To compete with Schwinn for the top spot in the sales race, they signed up celebrity endorsements. In the 1920s, Shelby employed aviator Charles Lindbergh to market the Lindy, a standard-frame bike that had a fender ornament in the form of Lindy's plane complete with free-spinning propeller. In the mid-1930s, they sent a truckload of balloon-tire bicycles to South Bend, Indiana, and presented them to the Notre Dame football team, receiving an endorsement from Knute Rockne in return.

As the market for bicycles heated up, and as American society became more influenced by news and advertising media, publicity became more important to bicycle manufacturers. While Shelby funded and equipped a racing team in these years, it was Schwinn that got the most mileage from its association with the heroes of the velodrome. A new form of six-day racing—"team sixes" with two-man teams alternating

Letourneur Paramount, 1941 (reproduction)
Arnold, Schwinn & Co., Chicago
Schwinn promoted the Paramount and other lightweights with professional racing, and in 1941 sponsored Alfie Letourneur's record-setting speed of 108+ miles per hour with a special cycle and a midget race car drafting. These efforts never created the big adult market for bikes that Schwinn craved. That eluded American manufacturers until the 1970s.

Paramount prototype, 1937
Arnold, Schwinn & Co., Chicago
Emil Wastyn, Chicago

Schwinn's desire to promote lightweight bicycles for adults was a long and expensive undertaking. In 1937, Frank W. Schwinn worked with race mechanic Emil Wastyn to fashion a cycle with chrome-moly tubing and high-end components. Schwinn also created a six-day race team for the Paramount, which won consistent praise as the best bicycle made in America. The Paramount name represented Schwinn's pride and joy for decades. Its lug frame was considered a masterpiece of the cycle maker's art, and basic construction changed little until the Schwinn company was sold by the family, and the Paramount tradition migrated to Wisconsin-based Waterford, founded by Frank W.'s grandson, Richard Schwinn. (Photographed with the Ignaz Schwinn Trophy, amateur racing's biggest prize in the late 1940s.)

shifts around a big banked track—was one of America's biggest professional sports at the time. Movie stars joined politicians and gangsters in the box seats every evening at races in America's biggest cities. With this kind of excitement, bicycle manufacturers did what they could to regain the glory days of racing in the bicycle boom.

For the manufacturers, racing was an expensive proposition, but they made the investment because they believed in something else from the old days: the market for adult lightweight bicycles. Lightweight sales were not impressive at the time, but companies like Shelby, Columbia, and Schwinn never gave up on the idea that adult riders were out there and waiting. Frank W. Schwinn went so far as to commission what became the best-made American racing bicycle of the era, the Paramount, designed and built of high-end tubing and aluminum components by a Chicago bicycle mechanic named Emil Wastyn.

Wastyn was highly regarded by six-day racers, so it was natural for a high-profile team to figure into Schwinn's marketing plan. In the late 1930s, many of America's best racers were riding Paramounts and wearing Schwinn jerseys, including Bobby Thomas, Jerry Rodman, Jimmy Walthour, Al Crossley, and Cecil Yates—some of the best-known professional athletes of the period. They rode in New York, Chicago, Detroit, and elsewhere against some of the bicycling world's biggest names from Germany, Italy, and Holland.

A measure of national pride figured into the Paramount's success. By early 1939, for example, a big Cleveland race was won by Walthour and Crossley, which "marked the first time in about 30 years," reported the *American Bicyclist* magazine, "that an all-American team won on Made-In-America bicycles." Political tension even helped make the Paramount a *cause celebre*. While good riding by any racer was admired, patriotism prevailed at a 1940 race in Chicago when a German team was booed off the track for riding the final legs of their winning race with what looked like swastikas on their arms.

As a result of the six-days, the Paramount became well-known as the most expensive bicycle on the market—something like $100 at the time. Schwinn advertised them enthusiastically, along with some lesser Schwinn lightweights, the Superior and the New World. Dedicated bicycle tourists also revived the long-moribund League of American Wheelmen at this time. But the lightweight market made little progress before World War II turned the focus of American industry. The market would eventually come to adult cycling in great numbers, but it would take time. Patience, fortunately, was another quality of Frank W. Schwinn that helped make his "lightweights" an eventual success and his company one of the most dominant in any industry in the mid-twentieth century.

Chapter 3
Postwar Classics

Before World War II, youngsters teamed up with manufacturers to save the bicycle industry from oblivion. Kids took to balloon-tire beauties like dogs to puddles. "Depression-be-damned" was the attitude of the companies that produced a dazzling array of now-classic bicycles all through the 1930s and right up to 1941.

The war represented a turning point for this industry as it was for many aspects of American life. It was certainly no golden age for bicycles, rather a "spartan" period with the few models turned out intended for critical employees of war-production factories

Schwinn produced a good wartime Cycletruck, used to deliver mail at Navy installations. Columbia produced a line of heavy balloon-tire models, hulking and painted a dull shade of green. Naturally enough, Columbia chief executive Edward Clarke used wartime austerity to promote the idea of lightweights for the government.

But military-style conservatism dictated balloon tires, so the opportunity to develop a new population of adult cyclists fell on deaf ears.

What the war did for the bicycle industry, instead, was create enormous pent-up demand. Combined with the coming baby boom, the balloon-tire cruiser market was about to surge as never before. By 1947, an unheard of 2.8 million bicycles would be sold, and the makers of Schwinns, Shelbys, Rollfasts, and Roadmasters were about to play their part in the largest economic expansion in the history of America.

The industry's objectives were a little different during this period than they were before the war. The sheer volume of production now demanded a more standardized product, and for this reason, postwar bikes featured less innovation and fewer examples of pure design flair. Bicycles became more conventional and predictable,

Victory Sports Tourist, 1942
Columbia Manufacturing Co., Westfield, Massachusetts
Columbia's president Edward Clarke was pushing to build unlimited supplies of lightweights like this one and put America on bikes for the duration of the war and beyond. It didn't happen, unfortunately, and a nation of cyclists was still a thing of the future.

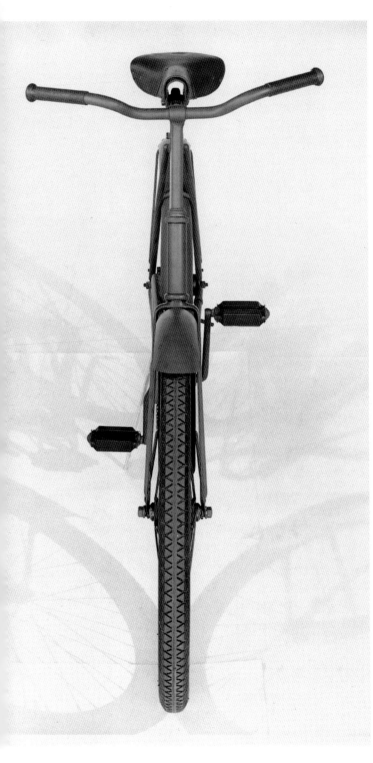

originally because they could be turned out more quickly, but eventually it was because their very sameness made them necessary to the growing army of dedicated consumers.

Manufacturers got to know their customers with all the skill that "marketing science" could muster. They learned, for example, that baby boomers may not have cared much about original art-deco lines and profiles, but they loved accessories. Headlights, reflectors, horns, and handsome new suspension systems were called for.

Every manufacturer worth its salt embraced the idea of "planned obsolescence." In cars, appliances, and countless other consumer products as well as bicycles, different models came yearly. Brook Stevens, a designer at Roadmaster, defined the concept as "better, more desirable products each season so the customer can't resist upgrading." It was true. Superficial changes in bike design came fast and furious during this period.

Schwinn, still led by the visionary Frank W. Schwinn, remained the postwar leader, and its biggest winner came in 1949 with the Black Phantom. This glimmering steed represented no real innovation, but it led the market in desirability for years. Black Phantoms proved that cantilever frames and "knee-action" spring forks were basic necessities in good neighborhoods.

Army bike prototype, 1942
Arnold, Schwinn & Co., Chicago
The kinds of bicycles built for wartime service were based on what the bicycle manufacturers had mastered in the 1930s. Balloon tires were tried, true, functional, and well adapted to the Cycletruck (right). When the war was over, pent-up demand for bikes was all for balloon-tire cruisers.

They added a drum brake on the front, automatic brake light on the rear carrier, and other features of an imaginary motorcycle. But most of all, the Black Phantom had chrome—chrome fenders, chrome rims, and chrome on the tank. Schwinn understood that what automakers were providing, which was chrome galore, was what bike riders wanted as well.

Glitz, not guts, sold Black Phantoms (along with a couple of not-too-risky variants, the Green and Red Phantoms). America was entering the Eisenhower years, the age of conformity, and because of good quality and even better advertising, Schwinns became lionized by children everywhere. Quickly phased out were the Excelsior head tag and other private labels, as Schwinn became a status symbol to a generation that would later go after BMWs and Calvin Klein.

Other manufacturers wouldn't admit it, but their main objective was to keep up with Schwinn. In doing so, they introduced ideas of their own, some of them quite different and destined to become the desirable classics of today. The Roadmaster

Schwinn Cycletruck, ca. 1940
Arnold, Schwinn & Co., Chicago

Black Phantom, 1954

Arnold, Schwinn & Co., Chicago

The Black Phantom became the icon of kids from 1949 through most of the 1950s. Authorized dealers, advertising, and good quality gave Schwinn a reputation among the kids that no one else could match. The Phantom won children's hearts with chrome, chrome, and more chrome. Red and Green Phantoms were available for kids to express individuality, but the Black Phantom was king of the playground.

Luxury Liner was one. In the past, its maker, Cleveland Welding Company, built chain-store bikes, nothing much to speak of in terms of style or quality. But the rise of more discerning youngsters led to the hiring of designer Brook Stevens, who provided some fancy ribbed chrome detailing, a stylish headlamp, and incorporated a "Shockmaster" front fork. Stevens improved the Roadmaster year by year and little by little until 1952, when the Luxury Liner represented a kind of adolescent climax. It combined a new rear brakelight, bowed struts billed as "crash bumpers" around each wheel, and a suspension system that rivaled Frank Schwinn's "knee-action" job.

Another memorable entry of the era was the Huffy Radiobike of 1955. This short-lived classic had a car-sized radio in the horn tank and a dry cell battery riding conspicuously on the rear carrier. The idea came from Horace Huffman Jr., then a young man who often counseled his father in baby-boom styles, and who imagined a childhood version of automotive luxury in the Radiobike. It was successful for only a year, however, as the transistor radio, appearing in 1956, made the Huffy's large antenna and heavy "Power Pak" quite obsolete.

Consumer society moved quickly in the 1950s, and many different forces were guiding American tastes. Among the most important was the rise of California and the entertainment industry. For manufacturers, this led to completely new design decisions, such as transforming a bike into a horse. This was what Rollfast did, or tried to do, in its Hopalong Cassidy model, an elaborate Westernized two-wheeler with saddlebags, studs, and "frontier fringe." Holster and pistol were attached to the stem. Hopalong was a big star in the 1950s. A 24-incher with his name on it enabled kids to identify with the cowboy and buy a bike at the same time.

Another theme bike from the postwar period came from Shelby, which now had a plant in California, not far from the soon-to-be-popular Disneyland. Shelby's marketing personnel had foresight enough to know that Disney's Fantasyland characters would maintain a durable hold on kids, and the result was the noble Donald Duck bicycle, which looked like a duck, quacked like a duck, even had fenders that tailed-out like a duck. It was actually a 24-inch bike for kids that sold very well for a few years after it was introduced in 1949.

The bicycle market continued to grow, but not in a regular and easy-to-master fashion. New riders were coming to the bicycle every day, and old riders were upgrading their vehicles like junior social climbers. They were a moving target. Early on, balloon-tire bikes were the holy grail. But as riders got older, their imaginations required new stimuli. Higher speeds would do.

Something faster was coming: lightweights. For American manufacturers, lightweights were an old song, as they'd been trying to get them on the market for a long time. They had little success before the war, and now as adolescent riders looked ready for a faster ride, the companies were faced with something else: European competition and the so-called "English racer."

The economics of the imports were hard to fight. Postwar Europe was ravaged

and the nations were desperate for foreign exchange. Bicycles could and did generate revenue, and their invasion of three-speeds, handbrakes, and thin tires began around 1951. Prices were as low as $30 per bike, and by 1955 the English, French, and a few others captured 1.2 million of 3 million bikes sold in the United States that year. This was an unpleasant reality for American companies, which had two strong responses. One was to petition Congress for tariff protection, declaring its "confidence in President Eisenhower . . . that no American industry will be sacrificed for international trade." But the manufacturers never did get what they wanted.

The industry's other response was more positive. As it kept its eye on the underlying causes for the imports' success, which was the market's desire for lighter bicycles, the Americans chose not to compete directly with the Europeans. Instead, they created a new trend all their own, and by 1955 they had begun the era of the middleweights.

It worked almost immediately. As the heavier cruisers were unsuited for older kids traveling greater distances, middleweights were the next logical step in the industry's planned obsolescence, which rivaled mutual assured destruction as a keynote theory of the Eisenhower years. Middleweights were a

Monark, 1948
Silver King Manufacturing, Chicago
The need for standardized bicycles to meet the surging postwar demand didn't mean that elegant bikes were a thing of the past. Monarks featured the normal conventions of the day—long wheel base, rear carriers, and front suspension—but in this top-of-the-line model, they did it with a bit of style that suggested some inspired designers were left over from the 1930s.

Huffy Dial-a-Ride, 1950
Huffman Manufacturing Co., Dayton, Ohio
In a period when rideability sometimes seemed less important than bulk and accessories, the Dial-a-Ride provided a small feature reputed to enhance functionality: a knob atop the front suspension could soften or stiffen the spring depending upon neighborhood terrain or the personal riding style of the operator.

compromise—bikes with narrower tires but curb-crunching durability.

The most famous middleweight of the period was the Corvette, introduced by Schwinn with plenty of fanfare in 1954. This model combined a long list of desirable features, including 1-3/4-inch tires (as opposed to 2.125-inchers) and "New Narrow" design.

Named boldly after the sports car introduced the year before, Schwinn's Corvette came with accessories such as handbrakes, three-speed rear hub, European-style saddle, fancy-looking headlight, and "rat-trap" carrier on front.

Traditional Schwinn construction got equally high billing. "Middleweights lead a

Bowden Spacelander, 1960

Bomard Industries, Grand Haven, Michigan

English auto designer Ben Bowden conceived the Spacelander in metal. After its introduction at a prestigious design exhibit in London, it was produced in fiberglass. The Spacelander had a lot going for it: it was lighter than most balloon-tire bikes, and it had the sealed and aerodynamic look of interplanetary travel. But 1960 was smack in the middle of the age of conformity, and Spacelander didn't look like a normal bike. So much the better for today's collectors who believe only about 500 were made and are willing to pay up to $5,000 for a Bowden.

Whizzer and Whizzer motor, ca. 1950s

Whizzer Motor Co., Pontiac, Michigan

Whizzers had a wartime permit to manufacture home-front consumer products because they could provide transportation with minimal gas and rubber. By the late 1940s, the Whizzer was producing the full bike with special frames and mounts. Whizzers were big until the mid-1950s when accidents started taking their toll and state governments ruled that this was driving, not riding. Licensed drivers preferred cars.

Phillips Cycles catalogue

Phillips Cycles of England was representative of the European makers that were able to flood the market with "racers" in the postwar economy. They confounded American manufacturers in two ways: they created a new taste a for faster ride in what had been a happy era of fat-tire bicycles, and the European models were inexpensive. The Excelsis (pictured above) was a fine bike that carried a list price of $34.50 after the war.

Huffy Radiobike, 1955

Huffman Manufacturing Co., Dayton, Ohio

This was a more advanced version of the bicycle's motoring fantasy. The horn tank was now a dashboard of sorts, and the battery on the rear carrier certainly indicated something modern and powerful beyond the mechanics of a mere bike.

double life," advertising declared, and it worked. By 1955, at some bike shops, 60 percent of total sales were middleweights. "The easiest way to sell a middleweight is to let the kid take it out and ride it and also let him ride a lightweight," said a dealer in Grand Rapids, Michigan. "After riding both, the kid will tell you the middleweight rides just as easy."

Corvettes were good bikes, but the effort to sell them was even better. Schwinn's authorized sales network became an important part of the bicycle story of the era.

Developed before the war, Schwinn's selling techniques were modeled after a California bike dealer, George Garner, who convinced himself, and then the rest of the industry, that the traditional bike shop needed an image transplant.

Garner, a former employee of Hans Ohrt in Beverly Hills, went out on his own in 1947, first in the growing San Fernando Valley and later with four additional stores in the L.A. area. Garner learned what Ohrt knew: professionalism worked, and not just with the silk stocking trade in Beverly Hills.

Roadmaster Luxury Liner, 1952
Cleveland Welding Co., Cleveland, Ohio
Roadmaster had been building cruisers for several years by the time Cleveland Welding took its best-riding design, inlaid it with chrome galore, and emblazoned it with a word that normally described cars or trains: luxury. The Luxury Liner didn't look too different from the Black Phantom. It was a high-end consumer product that was a very big deal just to own. Today, it is remembered with enough nostalgia that Roadmaster, now a Brunswick Corporation subsidiary, has come out with a reproduction for aging boomers.

Garner trained his mechanics, put them in clean aprons, and they doubled as salesmen.

Schwinn upgraded the image, and with Garner, he refined selling almost to a science. They invented what they called the "total-concept" store, and taught the Garner lessons all over the country. Sales talks were rehearsed. Technical schools were traveling road shows. It changed the way bicycles were sold. Before long, the best 15 percent of the stores were selling 90 percent of the bikes, and Schwinn's

percentage of the market, already large, peaked at 26 percent in 1956.

Another sign of the changing times in the bike industry was a product that made a very interesting splash for the better part of the 1950s. It was the Whizzer, a cross between bike and motorbike, which got jump-started during the war when light-duty motorized transportation was a necessity.

The original Whizzer product was a $90 four-cycle engine, which could be mounted on most balloon-tire bicycles. Later, the

Donald Duck bicycle, 1949
Shelby Cycle Co., Shelby, Ohio
Gene Autry Westerner, 1950
Monark Silver King, Chicago
Bicycles had been massaging the imagination for a long time. It was only a matter of time until Hollywood joined forces with the two-wheeled industry. For Western tastes or Disney-style innocence, kids could express themselves through characters on the silver screen and TV.

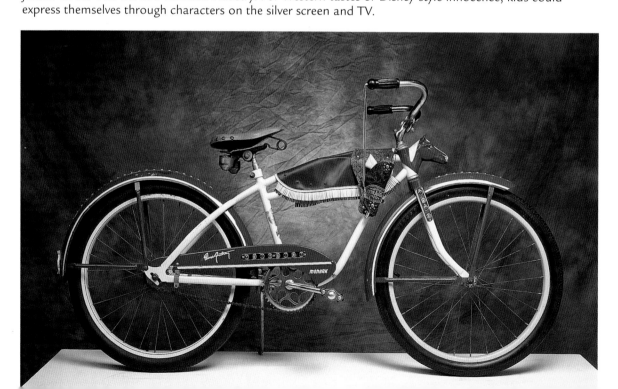

Sears Spaceliner, 1965
Murray Ohio, Cleveland
The space race was on, and Sears Roebuck sold the most rocket-like bicycle ever. The Spaceliner had a minimalistic "jet sweep" tank. Its abundant chrome gave it the look of lightness and speed. Neat as they were, Spaceliners had a short run of popularity. Baby-boom consumers, a constantly moving target, were about to shift to Krates and 10-speeds.

company assembled and sold completed bikes. For postwar, pre-driving age kids, the Whizzer became a big deal. The Whizzer company was often in financial trouble, but it still acted like a big-time manufacturer. It advertised in all the right places—*Life*, *Popular Mechanics*, and the *Saturday Evening Post*. When it got into patent-infringement trouble with Schwinn over cantilever frames, it ingeniously solved the problem by producing a complete model with Black Phantom frame for sale in Schwinn stores.

The late 1950s produced some other classics. The middleweight Sears Spaceliner featured the lines of a rocket ship, or so it was assumed. There was also the peerless Bowden Spacelander, a fiberglass *pièce de resistance* fashioned by a British auto designer who won serious design awards in Britain for the work. Despite the fact that these bikes suggested outer space, neither had a big impact on the consuming public.

Maybe the Spaceliner and Spacelander were too late. Maybe the public was fickle about anything not advertised in four-color magazines, as these were not. In any case, they arrived on the edge of a new decade, the 1960s, when America was ready for radical change—at least as long as it came from a well-known manufacturer with both feet on conservative *terra firma*. That manufacturer was, once again, Schwinn, which was on the verge of two very big trends in bicycle chic.

Chapter 4
Muscle Bikes, Speed Bikes, and a New Boom

Bicycling's center of gravity had been moving west all along. American bicycles began in Boston with Albert Pope. Then they found a home in Chicago with Schwinn. By the 1960s, the newest ideas for bicycles were coming from California.

Maybe it was the weather. Most Californians enjoyed an endless summer, and outdoor activities could proceed uninterrupted 12 months of the year. California was also a place for new lifestyles, and if the history of American cycling had shown anything, it was that cycling was a way of life.

So it was that a new bike boom showed signs of life in the late 1950s with a small core of racing enthusiasts such as George Koenig and Rick Bronson. They were a pair of Northern California teenagers who found complete romance in the solitary pastime of cycling long and hard on the open road.

There were few races for Koenig and Bronson to enter locally, but they trained like they were preparing for the Tour de France. When they weren't climbing the torturous hills or sprinting along the flat parts of the peninsula south of San Francisco, they were hanging around the few serious-minded bicycle shops in the area. Palo Alto Cyclery was one, not far from Stanford University where Koenig's father taught. Cupertino Bike Shop was another. The kids read cycling magazines and carried on endlessly about gear ratios.

As teenagers, Bronson and Koenig developed rock-like quadriceps, but their imaginations went soft right away. As part of their passion for cycling, they went through a distinct Italian phase, demanding, among other things, pasta at every meal. Bronson named his cat Fausto after road-racing great Fausto Coppi. (Bronson was a model for the writers of the 1981 movie *Breaking Away*.) By 1958, the two young men packed their European bikes for Italy and entered a series of Italian races around Milan.

When they returned to California, Koenig, Bronson, and a few of their friends started a local cycling club and called it Pedali Alpini, loosely modeled after Italian

Sting-Rays and Krates represent the fondest dreams of any bicycle designer. They became runaway best sellers in bike shops throughout America in the 1960s and early 1970s. Today they are coveted by collectors because they evoke a simpler time when kids had the run of their neighborhoods and life's biggest dangers seemed to be a wheelie gone bad and the oversized stick shift on the cross bar.

Pedali Alpini training, ca. 1959
In the late 1950s and early 1960s, the Pedali Alpini modeled themselves after Italian junior cycling clubs and helped bring road racing to Northern California. At first, these riders, Bob Tetzlaff and George Koenig, had few places to compete. Little by little, they found races in California and eventually made the 1960 U.S. Olympic Team.

racing teams. For several years it was not uncommon to see them, in green and white jerseys, riding single file and abnormally fast throughout the peninsula. As they got older, they traveled around the state and the region to races where they tested their mettle. Then in 1960, Koenig traveled to Rome as a member of the U. S. Olympic team. Bronson found his way to Italy by studying classical archaeology.

Little by little, the Pedali and growing numbers like them made racing bicycles with derailleur gears and down bars popular and even fashionable. Racing bikes had never really disappeared, of course. Racing still had its hot spots in places like Newark, with race mechanic Pop Brennan, and Chicago, where Emil Wastyn's son Oscar had a small but devoted following among racers. But it was in California—with Hans Ohrt in Los Angeles and retired six-day racer Oscar Juner in San Francisco—where new kids were coming from the ball fields and probably detention halls to ignite interest that grew into the next bicycle boom.

One of those boomers was Peter Rich, who was an adolescent from Oakland in the

Varsity, 1960
Arnold, Schwinn & Co., Chicago
As road racing increased in popularity in the West, word reached Chicago, where Schwinn was ready to produce the Varsity, one of the biggest-selling American bicycles of all time. Initially, it was an eight-speed and the lever to shift the front derailleur was low on the seat tube.

1950s when he received a new middleweight as a gift. Instantly intrigued, he took it apart and reassembled it several times before he realized his friends at school thought bicycles were square. But by then he was hooked, so he started riding across the Bay Bridge to join older racing types who gathered at Oscar Juner's American Cyclery, and trained on an old bicycle track in Golden Gate Park. Technically inclined, Rich went ahead and combined a three-speed derailleur set with his internal three-speed hub. The result was a slow nine-speed and a complete fascination with the possibilities of bicycles.

Peter Rich was not the only bicycle convert of this sort, and the manufacturers and sellers were noticing. Schwinn in particular had been angling to sell adult lightweights for a long time, so when California whole-sale distributor Bob Wilson started talking about derailleur gears, the Chicago company was naturally skeptical, but they were ready. In fact, Schwinn had tried an eight-speed derailleur model in 1952, though sales proved non-existent at that time. Now, despite a thousand derailleur sets still gathering dust in the factory, Schwinn got its soon-to-be-famous ten-speed (initially an eight-speed) Varsity quickly into production.

By the 1970s, road racing had ignited an explosion in touring. While down bars were once considered strange, they became common on the streets and roads of America, despite the leisurely nature of most cycling.

In Schwinn parlance, the Varsity was a "speed bike," but that was an exaggeration. Heavy-gauge steel, thick enough for standard welding, was the order of the day, and the durability mindset at Schwinn only started with the frame. Early Varsitys used various French derailleur sets, but they tended to malfunction under the less-than-delicate use of most Varsity riders. Eventually, Shimano made its biggest move to date on the American market when it designed an all-steel derailleur with sealed bearings in the freewheel, intended to foil youngsters who apparently were riding their ten-speeds through sand pits.

The ten-speed movement gained momentum in the United States, though it did little to benefit the Schwinn Paramount, already a classic and highly coveted by the few who really knew racing. Ever since 1939, Schwinn had been manufacturing and promoting it. Unfortunately, the Paramount never had the mystique of Cinelli or Bianchi, but Schwinn kept at it and maintained the worthy tradition of high-end American frame-making.

The Paramount's influence was felt particularly in California, where the torch had been passed to Albert Eisentraut, a native Chicagoan who learned the art of the bike frame in the shadow of the Wastyn and Schwinn craftsmen. When Eisentraut moved to California in the 1960s, demand for his custom-made masterpieces was low but sufficient to keep him busy.

Shortly after getting started in the Bay Area, Eisentraut hooked up with Peter Rich, who had recently opened a bike shop, Velo-Sport, in Berkeley. With the two of them, serious cycling seemed to be on a fast track. Not everyone could afford a $400 Eisentraut frame, certainly, but appreciation for the exotic metals, precise geometry, even the fine paint on a performance bicycle was on the rise.

Racing reached a new high point in 1971 with the inauguration of a race called the Tour of California, a 685-mile staged race between San Francisco and Squaw Valley, which attracted 70 serious riders. This

Paramount, 1980s

Arnold, Schwinn & Co., Chicago

Road racing grew in popularity in the 1980s, as did the Schwinn Paramount, a world-class racing bicycle. Despite (or because of) enormous resources poured into the Paramount, it never turned much of a profit for Schwinn, which would declare bankruptcy in the early 1990s.

tour had the festival atmosphere of a big French or Italian event. Rich did what he could to overcome the dislike that most police had for cycling at the time. Contact with of the head of the California Highway Patrol helped. At one point, the race had to ride right through a half-hearted roadblock near Stockton. Racing had attained critical mass.

The Tour of California did not last as an annual event, nor did Eisentraut's collaboration with Rich. But they represented important turning points, because they brought a new generation of enthusiasts to the true charms of cycling. Bicycle culture was percolating and definitely on the rise when another event took place that would catapult bicycles firmly into a boom stage.

It was the 1973 Arab oil embargo. It seemed like a global disaster, and cycling looked like a solution. It instantly swelled sales of Varsitys and the slightly more expensive Schwinn Continentals, which had

71

Sting-Ray, 1964

Schwinn Bicycle Company, Chicago

The Sting-Ray started in 1963 as a simple 20-inch frame with a polo seat and ape-hanger handlebars. By the next year, it was a phenomenon that offered this souped-up model with factory-spec windshield, front spring fork, and even a two-speed "kick-back" rear hub. This one was restored by Hyper-Formance, an Arizona specialty parts supplier.

aluminum stems and rims. It also got other American makers into ten-speeds and brought truckloads of Raleighs, Peugeots, Motobecanes, and Asian makes into the country. Some bikes didn't even make it into the shops as they were sold to eager customers right off the trucks.

The boom brought new enthusiasts, young and old, including names like Joe Breeze and Gary Fisher, who took cycling to heart. But before the mountain bikers of the world made their mark, something else developed—this for kids who didn't know a Cinelli from a jelly bean. It was the "muscle bike," also known as the "high-riser," ultimately the Sting-Ray. It became the biggest selling style of the 1960s by far.

Sting-Rays developed in an almost whimsical way. In early 1963, a Schwinn representative in Southern California returned to Chicago and said that "a goofy thing" was happening out there. You couldn't find a 20-inch frame anywhere, new or used, because kids were buying them up, putting polo seats on the back and ape-hanger handlebars on front. The result was something completely different, and the kids loved it.

This news came to Schwinn's vice president Al Fritz at a time when Frank W. Schwinn was near death in Chicago. Perhaps to get his mind off his boss's demise, Fritz was eager to try something new. He went back to the factory and found an old polo (also called "banana") seat, manufactured some years before by Persons-Majestic, which had never sold very well despite persistent efforts. Fritz also bolted the special handlebars on a 20-inch frame, and what he had was the first Sting-Ray.

Frank Schwinn passed away in the meantime, and when the company's most important distributors were in Chicago for the funeral, Fritz brought a few of them out to the plant to demonstrate his odd concoction. At first, they said it looked like a loser, but when they rode it around the paint shop, they felt differently. They found it handled with more agility than bigger bikes. And it was fun. Maybe it would work, they said, and they were right. For the remainder of 1963, the Sting-Ray sold 45,000 copies, and the only reason it didn't sell more was because the supplier ran out of 20-inch wheels.

What made the Sting-Ray such a success? Marketing was part of it, and by adding different features each year, Schwinn was practicing something like planned obsolescence on steroids. For the factory, it was easy enough. When Fritz and the designers thought up the Krate series—Orange Krates, Apple Krates, Pea Pickers, etc.—it was simply a matter of assembling what amounted to spare parts left over from earlier models. The front spring fork had the same machining as the old ballooners. Abuse-resistant derailleur gears had been developed for the Varsity. The 16-inch front wheel was a standard item, as was the drum brake.

For kids, it all had strange and wonderful power. The marketing muscle of Captain Kangaroo, a long-time Schwinn spokesman, naturally helped. But mostly it was the magic of a bicycle that looked enough like a dragster and little enough like a bike to become an icon to at least half a generation of kids.

Krates, 1968–1973
Schwinn Bicycle Company, Chicago

Orange Krates, Apple Krates, Lemon Krates, Cotton Pickers, and others (like Grey Ghosts and Pea Pickers) used a variety of parts that had other uses for other bikes. Front spring forks and drum brakes had been tooled in the Black Phantom days. New combinations of old features was a Schwinn specialty. Perhaps the most brilliant hybrid ever, Krates used a 20x2.1-inch tire in back and a 16x1.75-inch in front. The 1969 catalogue stated that this wheel configuration rendered the Krate with "styling similar to the racing cars found on drag racing tracks."

Today, newsletters and web sites relive the old days of Sting-Rays and Krates. Most of it is innocent nostalgia for the herds of neighborhood kids who rode down the street, each imagining he (or she) was driving a Corvette, a Mustang, or a Barracuda. There was danger, too. Evel Knievel was then threatening to jump the Grand Canyon on a motorcycle, and his fantasies were contagious. Soon kids were setting up ramps and trying to get up enough speed to clear the sand box or a stack of tires.

Sting-Rays attracted the bad boys, too, like one who later recalled in a Sting-Ray newsletter about using Sting-Ray handlebars as "flame throwers." It would be night, he explained, and a car would be driving slowly and unsuspectingly down a lonely street. The rider would pour go-kart gas in the hollow tubing of the handlebars, place his mouth on one end (a modified handgrip), light a match at the other, and blow with all due force. The wall of flame could easily extend across the road and certainly got a rise out of the motorist in question.

Mischief was a part of the Sting-Ray experience, it seems, though the bicycle was easily forsaken for cars and dates when the time came for them. Nevertheless, cars and dating (and marriage) could grow boring, too, which probably has a lot to do with the classic muscle bike revival that started in the early 1990s.

That's what one bicycle collector found out at a big auto rally near Detroit as he described on a Sting-Ray enthusiasts' website. For whatever reason, the collector brought a van full of muscle bikes to the fairgrounds where he and his friends ended up ignoring the cars and riding around all day. The bikes attracted attention and brought a few more aging baby boomers to a hobby that may be expensive (some rare models cost thousands) but nothing like an obsession for 409s and GTOs.

Many collectors have become true connoisseurs, and debates about the merits of various makes and models can sometimes develop into friendly but not-so-quiet fracases—such as this e-mail response, presumably from an irate adult Sting-Ray fan, to a website comparison of Raleigh Choppers (another high-riser) to Krates," wrote one:

I don't understand how you can say in your previous messages how the Krate/picker series are [the] coolest looking rides around, but riding qualities/comfort/handling in your opinion are terrible, and say you really do love these bikes. If you really do love these bikes you wouldn't say those kind of things about these works of art . . .

Such debate may seem out of hand. But it's heartstrings, not logic, that rule the flea markets, auction blocks, and anywhere else muscle bikes of the 1960s and early 1970s have risen from American junk piles to the status of American icon.

Chapter 5
Grassroots Technology: Mountain Bikes, BMX, and Beyond

Time has done wonders for old bikes. Some of the popular favorites of yesteryear have become coveted classics of today. People are paying enormous prices for classics that bring back lost memories and restore forgotten youth. Additionally, some modern-day classics were losers in decades past but are now highly desirable as examples of what might have been. In either case, tens of thousands of dollars can be spent on the most authentic and sought-after models.

It's not just classic bikes that have gotten out of hand. The new bike market has grown beyond reason, too. What separates, for instance, a $5,000 bicycle from a $1,000 model? You may use space shuttle technology and shave a few seconds off your Sunday ride along the lake.

But . . . in the midst of irrational phenomena, there is order. Answers can be found in the history of bicycles, which is not an impeccable guide to the future, but it's the best one we've got. Should you spend two paychecks on a classic bike? . . . or a new one? Opinions will differ, but an understanding of streamlining is essential to any collector of classic bikes. Recent bicycle history (basically the story of the mountain bike), may provide lessons, too, because it is a case study of what's really important in a new bike as well.

If any bicycle of the last decade or two is destined to become a classic, it's likely to be an early mountain bike—the category that changed cycling and made America, for the first time, the epicenter of the bicycle industry. The mountain bike story is undeniably

The most modern bicycles of today are actually new versions of older ideas. Mountain bikes, which developed simultaneously in several different places, evolved from prewar balloon-tire bikes like this one ridden by Marin County, California, mountain bike pioneer Ray Flores, ca. 1977 (top). California was also the birthplace of BMX, a kid's sandlot sport which quickly became organized with teams (like these well-sponsored kids in 1982), uniforms, and some small bike companies that became big ones (bottom).

Redline Squareback with Moto Mag wheels, 1976
Redline Bicycles, Chatworth, California
In 1976, Mongoose's Moto Mag wheel was a must-have on the tracks of California. Combined with Redline's Chrome-moly tubular fork and a lot of other up-to-date BMX gear, a major new industry was emerging from the garages of BMX dads.

nostalgic. It involves a loosely assembled band of youngsters who liked to smoke pot and ride bikes on Mount Tamalpais in Marin County just across the Golden Gate from San Francisco. As teenagers, many of these innovators were dedicated road racers, but they were also more. They loved the outdoors. They loved bikes, and their adventuresome spirit had them riding up and down old fire roads on the mountain that was just about in their backyards.

There was no first mountain biker. In Marin County, some early off-road cyclists included a group now remembered as the Larkspur Canyon Gang, many of whom were San Francisco firemen who spent their off hours schussing down rocky trails from the top of Mt. Tam. They didn't consider themselves on the cutting edge of anything except, perhaps, serious injury. But they made a definite impression on a younger contingent from the area who were members of a road

Kuwahara B, 1984
Kuwahara, Japan
The Japanese got very excited about the potential of the BMX market. The Kuwahara had some race-worthy features, a handsome profile, and (its most saleable feature) a part in the big blockbuster movie *E.T.*

Schwinn Predator, 1984
Schwinn Bicycle Company, Chicago
Schwinn weighed in with some serious BMX equipment, such as the chrome-moly Predator, introduced in 1982. By then, however, kids were consumed by the Redlines, GTs, and Mongooses that were seen early and often on the big BMX tracks in Southern California. The once-leading bicycle maker of the world never really caught up.

racing group called Velo Club Tamalpais. The younger guys included Charlie Kelly, now a distinguished bicycle journalist, Joe Breeze, developer of the high-end Breezer, and Gary Fisher, who founded Gary Fisher Cycles. At first, notoriety or even gainful

employment was the furthest thing from their minds.

Somewhere along the line, the mountain bike pioneers went commercial. But before they did, they gave free rein to their passions about riding and finding the best

Freestyling, 1984
Freestyling was a trend of the early 1980s that didn't require organized races. The 1984 Predator (with mag wheels) found a niche in a market eager for something new and cool enough for Generation X.

things to ride. They also developed a taste for old bikes, but they found their favorites not in fancy shops, and certainly not at auctions, but in junkyards. It turned out that the best bikes for risking life and limb on the trails down Mt. Tam were old "clunkers," as they called them, that had been discarded from before World War II.

Specifically, these were old Schwinns from 1937–1941. They had, it was agreed, excellent dimensions: 2.125-inch tires, 26-inch rims, high bottom brackets, and they were nearly indestructible. Fancier components could be added, though some considered

The Mountain Bike Hall of Fame and Museum

The Mountain Bike Hall of Fame and Museum was founded in 1988 in Crested Butte, Colorado, where hitting the summer slopes on a two-wheeler grew out of a local taste for big old balloon-tire clunkers, or "town bikes," as they were called. Crested Butte is beneath Pearl Pass, a 17,000 mountain pass near Aspen, and which, beginning in 1976, was an annual excursion for serious mountain bikers. Here are a few of the museum's bicycles which chronicle the early history of a sport that's now in the Olympics. Many, not all, have been altered for improved performance, though the purity of original clunkers was obviously valued by the earliest mountain bikers.

1977 Breezer modeled after 1937 Excelsior

1955 Schwinn World, modified ca. 1980

Joe Breeze's 1937 Exclesior

1949 Schwinn Autocycle

1950 Schwinn Spitfire, modified by Gary Fisher in 1976

Charlie Cunningham's handmade aluminum five-speed, 1979

Crested Butte, Colorado, Town Bike

Gary Fisher mountain bike used by Joe Murray to win 1985 NORBA (National Off-Road Bicycling Association) championship

Vision Recumbent, 1994

Advanced Transportation Products, Seattle

Recumbents are clearly more efficient than conventional upright bicycles, but they've always been derided by the mainstream. Even in 1933, when a second-rank French racer showed up at an event on a "velocar" with an exaggerated wheel base, and when he started winning, it was determined that this was not a bicycle. More recently, recumbent cycles have appealed to members of the International Human-Powered Vehicle Association, and others have tried to market them. But despite serious engineering—such as this short wheel base for improved handling—the traditional bike trade finds them inelegant and very hard to sell.

changing anything on a true clunker to be a sacrilege. At any rate, when you came cascading down "Repack" (a trail so-named because it burned the grease out of your coaster brake and you had to "repack" it) nothing was as important as a frame you could trust.

Joe Breeze was just one of these mountain bikers who became a connoisseur of old Schwinns. Around 1974, for instance, he was nosing around a Santa Cruz bike shop and found a 1941 B. F. Goodrich, a Schwinn-built ballooner, that looked perfectly "dirt-worthy." He bought it for $5, and when he got it to the mountain, he noticed that the double top tubes gave it rigidity. Its almost-perpendicular down tube gave it quick handling.

Gary Fisher also found a Schwinn-built clunker with an Excelsior head tag, and it is said that he was the first in Marin County to put derailleur gears on the back, a drum brake on the front, and fingertip controls on the handlebars. He won some races on

Gold Rush, 1986

Easy Racers, Watsonville, California

A motor racing enthusiast, Gardner Martin, got interested in experimental human-powered vehicles when he saw a magazine article by chance. In 1986, he built a recumbent cycle with an aerodynamic Kevlar body to achieve a speed record. Martin's Gold Rush was ridden by racer Fast Freddy Markham and took a few high-speed spills before hitting the 65-mile-per-hour mark—a record without a pacing vehicle in front. Martin's commercial model has a stripped-down fairing and moves nicely, but is relatively unknown outside his circle of friends.

that bike—particularly the annual Repack championship, a home-grown classic from 1975 through 1983—and it led to the beginning of a technical evolution that would change bicycles all over the world.

No one was standing still. Around this time, Breeze was thinking of the next step. Joe had learned frame building from Albert Eisentraut some time before. This knowledge combined with his love of the mountain-inspired "Breezer No. 1" which he built with a chrome-moly frame and the geometry of another old bike—his 1937 Excelsior, which he found slightly better than his 1941 B. F. Goodrich. Technical developments came non-stop after that.

Raleigh M9000, 1996
Raleigh USA, Kent, Washington
Suspension is now reputed to spell the difference between a winning mountain bike and an also-ran. The "unified rear drivetrain" features geometry and pivot points to reduce "pedal-induced shock activation" but float over the bumps and rocks of the most challenging race course or remote mountain trail. Raleigh's theory was somewhat the same, but because patents are now as important in high-end cycles as they were in the Pope-Overman wars 100 years ago, the execution is much different.

Another milestone event for mountain bikes came in 1978 after the Marin County boys learned about some other fat-tire enthusiasts in Colorado. For quite some time in the mining and ski town of Crested Butte, where the locals made a virtue of the simple life, townspeople had found that old clunkers suited their transportation needs quite well. They also discovered that the bikes rode great on the ski slopes when there wasn't snow. This led, in 1976, to what became an annual ride over 12,700-foot Pearl Pass from Crested Butte to Aspen.

The Pearl Pass Ride was meant to be an almost satiric answer to a fancy motorcycle ride from Aspen to Crested Butte. But after it was written up in a counter-culture magazine that the Marin County group read, they joined the Coloradans for the 1978 ride. Pearl Pass instantly took on mythic importance.

Mountain biking grew quickly after that. Two California companies soon recognized the logic of upright bicycles with soft saddles; Univega and Specialized imported low-priced models, which sold briskly. By 1995, 63 percent of the 10.8 million bikes sold in the United States were mountain bikes. In 1996, mountain biking was introduced at the Atlanta Olympics, which made Charlie Kelly remember a remark he made years before: "An American would win the Tour de France before mountain biking ever got in the Olympics."

All of which has motivated designers to continue where Breeze and Fisher left off. And then some. Now the highest-performance bike builders are not talking about the frame but the fuselage. Suspension systems are being designed by MIT engineers.

Big-time mountain bikes cost twice what cars used to cost 20 years ago. But not quite gone, and never forgotten, are the muscular clunkers that started it all.

BMX, another cycling technology of the 1970s, has similar grassroots origins, though its evolution differs greatly from the Mt. Tamalpais story. "Bicycle motocross" began, so the legend goes, in a park in Santa Monica with a lot of kids on Sting-Rays. They were racing over humps and berms, and, as things do in California, the activity caught on and grew. It moved slowly at first, but then in 1971, a feature-length motorcycle documentary, *On Any Sunday*, opened with a montage of BMX riders gliding over dirt and flying against blue sky. The film suggested that this was a new generation of motorcycle riders and signaled the next massive surge in bicycles.

BMX was different from mountain bikes because adults got involved. The riders themselves were as young as 12 or 13 years old, so BMX dads and moms took an active role in developing what became an organized (maybe over-organized) sport. By the early 1970s, so-called sanctioning bodies were all over California, probably because there was money involved. As competition for top riders heated-up, Yamaha, for instance, spent $100,000 in 1974 to promote the Gold Cup Series in the Los Angeles area while it was also selling its Yamaha Moto-Bike, noted for some fancy shock absorbers in back.

At this point, every vacant lot between Ventura and San Diego was a potential BMX track, and the sport looked like a

Homemade mountain bike, early 1970s
Ridden by Charlie Kelly, Mill Valley, California, when the mountain bike pioneers were starting to imagine the perfect off-road machine.

good way for otherwise underemployed adults to make money. There were definitely some scoundrels out there, but there were other oldsters who created quite legitimately what became a major industry. Magazines started up, which was important because they were sold in bike shops all over California and made BMX hard for any kid with a muscle bike to ignore.

Kawasaki followed in Yamaha's footsteps with an aluminum frame in late 1974. Schwinn, to its everlasting regret, stayed out of BMX for several years, convinced that the sport was a liability disaster. But that provided an opportunity for the small cottage industries growing up around the tracks. Also in 1974, a BMX dad named Linn Kasten used his motorcycle frame shop to fashion tubular chromemoly forks and sold 200,000 forks in a year. By 1975, his company, Redline, was turning out full frame sets.

Winning was not the only objective among the riders on Repack, mountain biking's first race course. But in the old days, the 1970s, those who finished with the best times were honored with ribbons that were as homemade as their bikes.

Around the same time, another father, drag racer Skip Hess, figured that mag wheels might impress kids and provide some added strength. He was right on both counts, and his Moto Mags came out, also in 1974, selling millions of copies in just a few years and getting Hess's company, Mongoose, on its way. Still others went from tiny beginnings to big roles in the BMX game, and in no time, the whole sport was drenched in money. By 1979, there was a pro class and at least one of the

E-Bike Standard, 1999
The dream of an efficient and popular form of electric transportation for city streets has intrigued bicycle makers for a long time. The E-Bike, backed by Lee Iacocca, is one of a series of ambitious attempts to do for the electric mode what motorcycles did for internal combustion a century ago—with the basic bicycle as the essential intermediary of change.

S-Works FSRxc, 1999

Specialized Bicycles, Morgan Hill, California
Specialized Bicycles was one of the first companies to jump on the mountain bike trend and market it to a nation of new riders. The Stumpjumper—a bicycle based in part on the geometry of prewar Schwinn cruisers, as discovered in the 1970s by the Marin County bikers such as Joe Breeze and Gary Fisher—led to the S-Works FSRxc, which features an M4 alloy frame and suspension engineering that features the stiffness–softness combination that can't be achieved in even the most charming clunker.

top racers, a teenager, got something like $100,000 to ride for a manufacturer that built and sold BMX bikes for chain stores.

As bicycles enter the future, what's next? Metals have been refined to feather-lightness. Geometry is a high art. Suspension has benefited from more than 100 years of experimentation. Where can bikes go now? Who knows? Many people are trying to take the "invention" in different directions.

There are recumbents, for example, which are bicycles that enable the rider to sit in a supine position—more comfortable, potentially safer, and swifter than previous bicycle designs. Developers of this technology are absolutely convinced of its future. But the public seems less so. Experimental

machines using recumbency have broken speed records, and proved that pedaling efficiency is significantly increased on a recumbent. But something stands in the way. The innovation, in a word, is too eccentric. The same thing that worked against Bowden Spacelanders works against recumbents. Freakish? Maybe. Cyclists are purists. Maybe they're classicists, too.

Now there are electric bikes. Here, too, it's out of the ordinary. The EV Warrior—marketed recently by the likes of Lee Iacocca—may have a chance for popularity. It uses what looks like a traditional frame. Riders are upright. They can wave to friends. Maybe,

Allez M4, 1999

Specialized Bicycles, Morgan Hill, California
Slight variations on the traditional double diamond frame can be regarded as today's contemporary classics. In advanced road bikes, the high-tech touch at Specialized is in the M4 tubing, a metal with silicon, copper, magnesium, and vanadium content. This metallurgy enables extreme stretching and shaping for improved aerodynamics and increased strength where it's needed most (near the head tube, for instance).

just maybe, the bicycle will do for electric transportation what it did for internal combustion. A hundred years ago, the first motor vehicles were motorized bicycles, which were then, and remain, a fertile field for invention.

But so far, recumbents and electrics are minor trends. What's really new in bicycles is interest in old bikes. More than ever before, classic cruisers and other old two-wheelers are being dug out of barns and restored to the nines. They're also being reproduced by otherwise baffled manufacturers who don't know where the future of bikes is headed.

It all speaks well for the simple virtues. Cruisers or clunkers, or whatever they're being called, are very street-worthy indeed. In cities throughout America, nothing could be more common than seeing a stripped-down, even rusty, cantilever frame with a couple of fresh tires chained to a post, ready to take someone to work, to school, or even to the market. What they lack in lightness, they make up for in durability, versatility, and maybe even loyalty. You can put freewheels and derailleurs on them if you want. You can put big, soft, derriere-conforming seats on them for comfort.

It's as if the best ideas are the old ones. It is worth noting that one of the best things that happened to the bike business in recent years was a by-product of

Tetra-Tetra, 1999
Carbonframes Inc., Santa Cruz, California
Craig Calfee, a former art student, has embarked on traditional bicycle forms. His tandem uses new construction methods in old-fashioned geometry. Calfee's ultralight roadbike frames use a construction technique called "pressurized lamination."

Bamboo bike, 1999

Carbonframes Inc., Santa Cruz, California

Craig Calfee's bamboo mountain bike is a unique piece of work (reminiscent of the old hickory bicycles of yore) that achieves in natural materials, says Calfee, a measure of the strength and resiliency found in modern carbon fiber. Joints are laminated with adhesive and hemp that blends nicely with the natural tone of the wood.

Schwinn's exorbitant reproduction of the Black Phantom in 1995. When the new owners of Schwinn (the family company was sold out of bankruptcy in 1993) were getting ready to make the $3,000 repro, designers found Frank W. Schwinn's old plans in a basement. With these drawings, they didn't just make a limited edition that replicated the classic. They also applied some of the old geometry to a new line of modern Schwinn cruisers, and the bikes rode like a charm.

It goes to show that in the 1930s, 1940s, and 1950s, America had some very good designers working on bicycles. And in the midst of today's mania for classic

above: **Waterford 2220, 1999**
below: **Waterford Diva, 1999**

Waterford Bicycles, Waterford, Wisconsin

Waterford Bicycles represent the recent evolution of the Schwinn Paramount. Richard Schwinn, great grandson of founder Ignaz Schwinn, uses lug-frame construction and low-temperature brazing with the most advanced heat-treated alloy tubing. While Waterford frame sets are marginally heavier than carbon fiber, the precision in construction and alignment, says Schwinn, compensates for the sacrifice of a few ounces.

bikes—and for expensive high-tech bikes as well—it might pay to keep the tried and true in mind. Bicycles can take many different forms. They can have some uniquely handsome and innovatively useful features. But in the end, they operate with elegant simplicity. That's why the fine old cruisers were popular then and why they're popular now. More than likely, it's simplicity and elegance that will drive new discoveries—both collectible classics and hot new machines. And it's the bicycles that retain these qualities that will continue to be worth something in the future.

index